Cuttings from the Tangle

CUTTINGS FROM THE TANGLE

RICHARD BUCKNER

BLACK SPARROW PRESS · BOSTON · 2020

Published in 2020 by
BLACK SPARROW PRESS

David R. Godine, Publisher
Boston, Massachusetts
www.godine.com

LIBRARY OF CONGRESS CATALOGING-IN-PUBLICATION DATA
Names: Buckner, Richard, 1964- author.
Title: Cuttings from the tangle / Richard Buckner.
Description: Boston, Massachusetts : Black Sparrow Press, 2020.
Identifiers: LCCN 2020028383
ISBN 9781574232448 (hardcover)
ISBN 9781574232400 (ebook)
Subjects: LCGFT: Poetry.
Classification: LCC PS3602.U295 C88 2020 | DDC 811/.6--dc23
LC record available at https://lccn.loc.gov/2020028383

Cover Design: Milan Bozic

First Printing, 2020
Printed in the United States of America

written to be read aloud

CONTENTS

Chemtrails Across a Privileged Smog	13
Industry	16
NATIONAL PARK(S)	18
(*Fallen)	20
SURVIVAL	21
One More Last One	22
CO-OP COOP COUP	24
A Letter to the Words	26
FESTIVITIES	28
The Separating Circle	30
Up-against Until	32
VACATION	34
Beaten	36
ENFILADE	38
STORAGE	39
TAD'S	40
The Funeral Years	42
Apparently	44
Still	46
This was not expected	48
INDEPENDENCE	49
Premeditation	50
Assaulted while on a med run	52
in completion	54
CIRCUMFERENCE of a SINKHOLE	56
SLAKE	61
GHOST PARADE	62
Rest	64
Fumes	66

GET-TOGETHER   68

Chatterbox   70

as one   72

PASSING   75

The Thinning Apex   76

Oh, 00   78

bound   80

Everyone is driven unknowingly to their urges   82

(:)   84

Y   85

Work   86

Unknown, but for the Animals We Could Be   88

Free   91

Yield   92

Offering   94

high   95

STATION   96

TURNBUCKLE   97

FAULTY   98

Behind   99

Cuttings from the Tangle   100

Chemtrails Across a Privileged Smog

Unrestrained by the squalor of sentimental entrapment
      & sworn to stay sentenced,
      the congregation continues to hymn itself silly
      confabulating a lineage miscarried to more of the same
      children of children,
      disguised in disguise
      at unlit pageants of imagined-meaning
      chaperoned by pedigrees with hackles raised,
      crouched and growling where the steps lead
      neither down nor up

          only high away,
      wired as low tides crashing,
      burned-out on the porches of charter roadhouses
      singed by zealot mantras,
      militant by original sin,
      willingly led to industrial seaways of flared refineries
      engulfed in possession,
      watering down the scraps in soft-lite
      neighborhoods, rushing calmly
      through jagged straits the lost stroll,
      the swept-up maneuver
      and the destitute quietly read-in
      to the temperate elements all organisms search past
      for provisional shelter,
      where everywhere is the fray,

          cruising empty towns sponsored by hateful believers,
      green-lamped and gazing from behind
      before turning on streets named after turgid all-inclusives
      attempting to reframe the reflection of a malignant mole
      itching near the taint of popped-collar-revivalists
      welcoming crucifix-chokered worried brows,
      tank-t'd puffy lids
      and broken-nose piercers
      lilting with badass drama and dismissed interest

in the body-sprayed journey of sandaled testes
leaving drunk in courtesy vans,
ditching rhinestoned wrists
tossing back flavored shots that die whining
under sacrificial hair-lifts,
boring the apocalypse into bringing on the rapture

      early in the uncomfortably perfect evening,
as beach skippers park under night-fire curtains
buttressing narrow lanes of experiments in simplicity
with home-delivered marrow on ice
cherry-picked by donors and dogs-alike,
tonguing from eateries with costumed biker-toughies
who stay in territorial character
while heritage anthem veg-medleys score
sports précis jockeys and truncated auto ad celebs
flat-paneling beside neon brandings
above buzzing wide-loads swerving with to-go containers
past milestone vessels topped-off without tipping,
generational imposters
and expense account floaters
looking out from the bar over unplanned families,
unable to tell the shoats from the rutters
gulping midnight sweet teas
washing down their deep-fried blessings
in habitual conspiracy,
amassing at the fighting cage for replays of shame
eating violence.

Lodgings are loose and scabbing as the houseflies only crawl
      up the stairs, pacing
      all night, wondering too-late
      how it got to this, drowning in the glowing
      transmitted highlights of local galleria talent
      shows with open-carry infants fearing their futures,
      interrupted by farmer dating/hair loss sales forces
      plugging between tele-faith skits of devotional-athletics
      vested and sold on proxy-war pride pledges

    barked, while leaning with drinks
from smoking-floor balconies,
to the ganglia screaming to piss themselves below,
splashing in the closed pool of their choices,
given and already taken away,
near sorority saucers landing in a dust of dissolution,
threatening in smacked intonations
that later on there will be either fighting or fucking
before scattering like Daddy's-girl cockroaches
tapping out to spread the debris,
returning in a late blank to shared rooms
adjoined with bovine yell-slurred responses
no one will recall

    heaving in the morning,
when a breakfast voucher-fascist bullies geriatrics
only cackling along just so they can get to the bacon
before dying of mediocrity, rewarded
as a motel desk clerk crosses the monitored lot
to remind a vagrant that only registered guests are allowed
to pick through the garbage of the musty
hallways blocked by limping luggage carts delivering baby
food and beer while a slow-passing call reports
I can't run from the pain

    relapsing in moments drifting on no matter,
conserved within the spoiling prescribed burn preserve
with open palms of salvation reaching out from the fearscape,
smearing chemtrails across a privileged smog.

Industry

Who brought you here blanketed in bending light
indirectly blazing from the treasure's weighty brilliance
of innocent eclipses remaining,

patrolling the undermining empyrean terrain
deserted in colors left playing in the flume
conceived by drowsy gimlets only boring for a lift,

coughing on rocks gifted from lawless shafts?

I'll bet you dragged your woozy senses out
climbing up for tricked compliments found caving-in,

       to venture,

waved-on with the dismissal of vicious premises
lost in the distance
until passed-out-wasted on forgotten front lawns,

only carried inside once the beauties turned
in awe, chirping within their hollow bones,
bashfully honoring their own blushing shame

       by blaming the shaping clouds

stirring in the aftershocks, biting through the reins,
drawing on siphons
milking venom from pictures of honesty,

counting off bruised endings glossed-over

wincing in introspection,
doubled up in grandiose refusals,

blowing out the matches with soured candy-breath
whistling timeless gratitude into a presumptive wind
framing contoured dreams pinched awake to witness,

struggling with obvious strain,

      as late news,

arriving in eloquent estimates
sitting behind decorated silhouettes,

clarifying a fire to pour down the well
finally shown to jurors crisping on the closing petals,

insisting blood is just,

      when industry is let to truly do its thing.

NATIONAL PARK(S)

I'd been there once before on a whim beyond periphery,
but without your bearing, finality frames everything from
behind

>   (in an upstairs motel room, window curtain-bordered by
>   the shifting lights of a TV, illuminating the mystery of
>   interior treasons no longer isolated, unaware of its
>   display)

, returning ages later to test denial for your permission,
granted wholly, unspoken with poise and strength to a witness
in weak remembrance

>   (above the parking lot guard watching unregistered baby
>   blue press-ons breaking plans to make it through, just one
>   more flight of many ahead, detaching unnoticed and
>   remaining, for next-time to replace)

, casting off palettes of wonder watching the colors drink you in,
sharing what I couldn't taste umbrellaed from the unwelcome sun
expecting hail

>   (with endless u-turns leading to lobbies where old men
>   pressed in khakis and buttoned-downs stay silent as
>   tightly-pulled ballerina dos over swollen face and all-pupil
>   shift leg-to-leg while spilling out the details)

, assailing in early observation of charges on the way, arriving
unprepared on a pulled rug of worn hope, with tears drawn in
a bathroom stall

>   (lost in the rummage past the wrench for prescriptions
>   awaiting wash-out next to cutlery laid out on a coupon
>   page read as truth, expired but still scoured for anything
>   to pass the perceptions)

, on plates removed backhanded by flawed inspiration deciding
where dead signals quietly guess along the unfenced rim
of an eroding abyss

> (lying from the corners appealing to a reserved crowd
> traversing between schedules, living for adventure within
> their walls and playground admissions, schooled in the
> shimmering lure of what's to come)

, when the only reason we woke together to explore the dawning
trail is because I fell, toward your figure and not, into the unending
that departs, if commuted to stay

> (enveloped in the fragments of loose accommodation and
> brazen declarations withdrawn at the slightest breeze of
> judgment without approval-of, when defense is fuel and
> retardant alike.).

(*Fallen)

all of us are (*,) hunting the hidden where we know they'll be,

leaving respectlessly quiet, bristling as we stand (, *) out from

the gathering whose choice words have (*) their way, into each

other's collapsed swarms, back to where we were (*), lying in the

shared (*) blame of being, without reparation for living (*,) far

away from jeweled, whispering shutters, (*) open now while

concealing who they've shown (, *) off with the timid who rush

in to drag down the (*) wrecks above the night that passion will

renounce, over anything we admit, fighting back (,*,) as the clashing

hounds round up the risen buried in the (*) years no one could've

withstood while continuing on to stay, still (*.),

SURVIVAL

united, guzzling ahead,
teeth of knives
smiling a "Goin' somewhere?",
spittle snapping back a "Yeahhhhh…*prob'ly.*",
grooving ruts on last legs of resistance
from taut-leash perimeters
loosely enforced as sunrise awakens
to clean off the blood of closing time
shots pouring somewhere in the blackout
journey between wilted open-endings
followed beyond their wherewithal
when a slow decline is a step in any direction at all
in the slaughterhouse line:

    Weekenders
         resting & reloading, flexed with their gassy toys,
         chowing on responses in territorial rally, drifting
         down timeshare slopes in the prone distance of pigs
         hunting the feral merely embracing the end,
         distracted in consuming amusement within
         the shrinking atmosphere squeezed into a vacuum
         of compressed futility, standing in allegiance to
    good ole r & r.

But, why not when it's always amateur night, again
breaking thru the safety corridor, applying the brakes
pressed in staining class, winking at the spoilers
gouged into a hive, to listen, sipping
subversives on the rocks and stumbling
to a stagnant nocturne on the first-date of too few
broken engagements lying
on the surface of rising tides
exposing the guarded unguided,
trekking in succession still
questioning the bargains
made along the way,
gambled to survive

One More Last One

Highway construction signs redirect past off-duty after
-hours machinery toward a frontage road motel attached to a
diner/lounge

with stools at the bar seating crisscrossing dialogue under
televised sports and bygone hits. An older woman, part
of her blouse trapped between her bra and her belly,
slouches forward ordering *"one last one"*.

Two weathered brothers laugh & look each other in
the eyes as they talk in grainy cigarette timbres, trading
stories of worksite coffee, trailer-office liquor and what
their hourlies have done or drunk, on or off the job. The
bartender refills a bourbon for the brother with a belted
knife sheath and long single braid, then caffeine for the
other with a close cut and belt clip keys.

A younger woman, a niece and a daughter ending
her shift there, sits between the two, folding forward to
talk to a waitress in hushed exchanges while the brothers'
conversations veer around her, then leans back to join in
with them as the server leaves to take the dinner order
for a man huddled alone at the end of the bar who wants
"just meat—no veggies". The sheathed brother looks over
at the man, watching the interaction, then glances at his
other.

The happy hour closing bell rings and the brothers rise,
each pulling out their different brands of smokes, pinching
into their packs and stepping out in the night

to the small parking lot with two logoed company trucks
amongst the dusty sedans and compacts with bungeed trunks

ajar, garbage-bagged side windows or duct-taped bumpers of the
itinerant workers staying over. A few of the motel rooms have
half-opened doors with no movement inside besides broadcast
dancing lightshow flashes. A small grill slopes cold on a bent leg
in the middle of the dim walkway.

    The brothers light up and draw, touching shoulder to shoulder
but facing opposite directions as if on watch for something
approaching from anywhere, talking in low, serious tones about
the niece/daughter; her beauty and ability to recover; one brother
looking away while speaking, as the other, head turned chin to
shoulder, looks at the narrator while listening, both switching
poses as speakers change.

    Only the key clip brother returns, scooting his stool
and looking straight ahead, silent as the coffee is refilled and
the empty tumbler taken away.

    The no-veggie man glances at the young woman while
mumbling his tip-addition, lays some bills on the bar

and walks out, crossing the lot toward the rooms, turning to look as
a truck door slams and a lit butt dives to the ground in his direction.

    The trapped-blouse woman loosely swivels her head,
past then back at the bartender, raising index and middle
fingers together with *"Okay, one more last one."*.

CO-OP COOP COUP

We live-on not knowing
   our demands from inside
     the body, conflicted by senseless applause
     defensively answering hearsay

we live on, not-knowing
   those shoving ahead with high-handed anti-reflection
   absolution

we live on not knowing
   legacy underlings, knocking on screened doors
     well aware of what's seen behind
     the general makeup of the trade,
     oversold at the expense of substance,
     simply shading-in the missing
     hues of a forest's fevered dream,
     exempted-losses continuing the lien
     without even possibilities to loan
     old newbie-spirits who simply vanish
     into holes we are-as;
     fragile enemies cower-carrying-on,
     so vast,

       just digging ourselves,
        in,
       on not
      knowing we live.

We live-on not knowing
   longing, scattered upon facsimile banners flying as-is
     the wind running-out, stuttering canons
     rolling on sordid empty plains, leveled
     with trembling, scythes of ages "only-askin'…"
     the unfortunate reasons

we live on not-knowing
> : b-e-c-a-u-s-e
>> because of what our spilled premise clearly spells
>> out, crying

"we live-on", not knowing
> the site of a withering wreck, hiding
>> relics of "don't remember us yet; we're still alive!",
>> but of each other,
>> in a shiftless shape flattened on the road,
>> that hasn't-been itself,
>> left to spread in all directions at the sideshow
>> forgotten as everyday
>> events clamoring for undeserved attention-to,
>> that hope-killing mess with no one-bully
>> to back away from, thieving shut-ins with tired fists
>> pressed to a window,
>> never recognizing
>> here-in for anywhere else "…, we guess";
>> kicking away, proudly
>> floating, facedown on the surface
>> we live on, not knowing

> *we live-on, not knowing*
> *we live on not-knowing*
> *we live-on,*
> *not-knowing.*

A Letter to the Words

Dearest hint,

like a notice pushed under the door—
loosened from the midst of a collection,
you must've slipped out

in remiss, punctuating
vaguely when to breathe
somewhere within the fragments
  of the details missing
  right there on the page
  that may run-on to nothing.
  If I could only skip back
   or ahead
     where our turned corner
      used to be.

The words are surely lying
plainly but, guessing composition,
appear unclear

as if foretelling a past
subjunctively described in speculation,
left in a tangential present
  tense from the mystery
  of where they are, once headed,
  were what they now
  wanted to be saying;
   are still how
    they all
      beautifully

began. Could you pass another?
I need to know
how goes our story.

Sincerely,

unable to read into
what can't be written-off as just
a letter to the words.

FESTIVITIES

beginning already in the fryer,
plotting alongside another seasoned raptor
to jointly prey from a hotbed spitting with conspiracy,

privately grilling segregated cherubs,
where answers were lies of intervention-reforming attempts
to keep the immunized miracles toking up

to bully their entitled beliefs, unmasked in winter gear
worn-out at stolen recitals, humbly returning an aging jingler
years late with respectful apologies for any unintentional larceny,

eluding the heat on wrong-way date-night acquittals,
in-flight to the continental shelf stocked with plans
to split for last-ditch negotiations, destined to dead-end,

westward ho for a fistful of chuckles
until the spring plains sirened flatly from a suburban veranda,
where pious peelers and shell-shocked undertakers intermingled

on hors d'oeuvre trays of kitchen blow and weed rolls,
entertained by clogging siblings dancing a hide-&-go-seek can-can,
well-played searching for an over-celebrant found,

paddling south in a promotional shoehorn, drowning in retreat
drunkenly tripping onto a launch pad wig-fire blastoff
above a harmonica-felching frat bro,

the maar deepening with inflammation, deflating
from a pneumonic alcoholic must traveling to numerous run-ins
scrambling in failed departure, calling to warn

provincial drug pigs had picked up the sour scent of summer fête
grounding out while engaged on a can-do afternoon of race-duelers
lancing with their infections, loose as a tweaked wedding band

detuning the inevitable harvest of future annulments, barely beating
an ambush within a congestion of cochlea, corndogging stage-to
-stage in a stampede of melodious gluttony as a hearty token lifted

to empty skies of closed canals draining with nowhere, pulling ahead
through purloined lands thick in the tangy sauce of fevered tradition,
silently approaching and shoving past amateur nationals snorting

useless salutes, as autumn intersected the fall of yet-another spell with
a brief ceremonial, entrancing exhausted options to become forgiven
in the freeze, wrested by the freedom of festive restraint

The Separating Circle

Found
under a twisted charm
bracelet still-clasped within
a bin atop a hope chest
scarred with an overlapping-two
coronas of water stain *o*'s,
as in some *loose heirloom*
pulled out, slipping in
its frame of-then, held
up to a dust-ray light showing

      children, crowded around
      a lamb, in the bed of a Ranchero
      parked with its tailgate down
      draped in a victory banner
      partially showing off whitewalls
      against a *loo*ming coastline sunset.

      The lamb is wearing a rimless cap
      above a necklace bell,
      *loo*king blankly ahead
      as a boy parenthesis hands
      below the lamb's jaw,
      holding it still to face the camera.

      Two smiling girls wear straw hats,
      names sewn into the brims: Kay and Jean,
      with a third girl who has no thread-cursive
      calling; maybe it was *too* expensive
      or there wasn't enough time, perhaps
      forever the one catching up late.

A staged vase of mixed flowers
crowns the roof above rabbits
held gazing pink from the flash
behind two boys, arms hanging
down, empty: the bigger one, lost
in powerless thought;

the smaller other, tense as if brooding
for something to finally end,
appears to have a retouched aura
of trouble that could be
there already were individual secrets
in joined furtive promise.

Beyond the kids and car, a lone adult
smiles as he glances away,
responding to something in the distance,
behind a stripling with award ribbons
dangling from unbelted loops, staring
towards the lens, waiting to be dismissed,

but captured in the separating circle
surrounded by what's no longer.
"There you are.", rummaging-amongst,
nearly-recent-departeds misremember
under quaint shrieks bubbling
laughter-cries, petting strangers' mementos
as in some *goodbyes misunderstood*
so long ago, they can only go,
"What else did you find?" given away,
for reasons forgotten for a reason.

Up-against Until

He wasn't sure what she was up-against behind that cash register, handing back the change with a wrist tattoo of either broken heart halves or fighting scorpions, asking where he was headed and not what he was coming from,

but if he'd driven to the next town over from her truck stop part -time-until-school's-out-then-I-don't-know employ… :

invented as the open road leading away from promise,
an ongoing re-beginning in aborted orbit

accompanied by a wounded engagement
rambling unattached, courting comfort
and deserting early to sow a last straw

(pulled with a barbed afterword
of weeping exposure)

rinsed and dressed in sensitivity, resting feet out
the window in open-container assumption tipped
back with resigned approval fading with the air

(conditioning confession from a sprain
of passion)

sated in starry eyes proud with captured bohemian
wisp stumbling away from obligation near or far
-fetched in recited doses of verse desperation
indebted to mortality voiced from a coddled stray
yelping from a leaning porch

(in broken-celebration encore)

wasted on invited witnesses swept up in the show
trolled by a deadpan monologue on the hunt

to shuck the world thought only worthy to slurp in
loose tobacco smoke, laughing to no one but itself
inside a gathering caste of alphas reduced to playing
along, doing their part to keep the greeting line
going into collections with a scarring question
mark of pretended civility, targeting

then discarding discounted detritus left tearing on
a flesh pillow of mistaken-soul cologne, license
without limit for what will be would-be birds
flushed to be picked off in a staged cornfield
on a highway of prison roses, dead roots and other
diggings of justification and evidence thereof for how
they continually come to barely be

daydreamt possibilities of any tack at a random exit, so
fully lost presuming there is someone else who needs to be
held such

> (by we-all understudy saviors waiting in
> clipped wings with blind scopes aiming
> directly into an endless-yet-another concealed
> sun begging to be noticed as it wanes out
> of obligation to the mystery of adoration
> or unacceptable peace, conceived as any
> abstraction, like love; as all impulses are
> just weaknesses conned into action

in the misguided ghost-chase of deserved-happiness
pursued to its burning end....

Well, he would've found her close friends removed, bonfire
-beer-recalling their hometown good old times and wondering
what she didn't see through in that emptied load from nowhere,

clinging lax like some secondhand doll that she kept around because it
was something she thought wouldn't let her down until he finally
did.

VACATION

They travel in fast packs
on narrow trajectories crammed
into down-market getaways,

merging cruise-controlled
cocktails of inflated heredity
with flatulent hometown ties

loosened by the magnificence
of a descending climb
out to low-hanging return,

rolling-on as a fruiting body
digging into infectious attractions
exploring for bitter relief

over an underpass of unseen terrain
       (where stalled shoulders
       wait it out for a call
       with any inside news
       promising an early release

       back into the mean time
       so far, but for now
       weathering the bedlam
       crystallized into last options

       misting from windows
       lowered passenger-side,
       pacing half-hour vacancies
       forfeited in the traffic

just jamming along
in the rhythm between
rides exchanged
for a commissary fund);
all in everlasting temporary escape,

with heads bowing to avert the eyes
as temples pray to sacrifice themselves,
unbuckling the snapping belt

from commitments beaten back
by omens of ignited postures
coughing-up a family-friendly fare

admission without distraction
while in-keeping-within clusters
of help-yourselfist second-helpings,

no matter what: the convenient cost
of excursions to the bletting edges
only passing around the fixins.

Beaten

(When you know)
you're not going to win,
you flatten the pedal and take it to the far end of the arc,
with dead weight watching your back for whatever calls
out from the sky, directly opposite the blinding star
nearly passing to see

(what might exist,)
across the northern plains interstate of a window
down in the open mind of a spring evening, promising
anything to make everything happen at will, within
the wasted expectation of wishes just begetting-on,
the way it all can be taken or left

(without glancing,)
rearview foretold,
ahead of the emptiness
where you'll come
alone,

(continually entering)
rooms of strangers
not concerned with your protection, projecting comfort
as a city-glow in the distance can,
telling that they know where you're not going,
to admit strange persona, even getting even

(with nothing)
for wanderlust to hide, in
a warm breeze excitedly pointing out
the next frontage as the place where you'll lie
down with better company, overcoming cradle
-chasing echoes calling from the load-bearing beam

                       (merely cross-dreaming)
        it's assumed the burden of insight
        swinging back at the nightfall
            you've only now
                beaten

                    (when you know)
you're not going to win.

ENFILADE

it's never convenient, listening to the munitions of daylight
-disobeyed, striking a vein pulsing-cold beneath the bed, ridden
home steadily seeking eventual release but merely putting you on
        night watch—
        shot-portioned scope of mason jar binocular cubes,
        proven as bottomed-out prairie wells
        drying up but fixable in the excessive remainder,
        juggling unscheduled carryover junctures
        too early for the hour to be happy,
        soberly removing the card-housed
        virgin liters sitting plump-within and cocky on
        the kitchen counter, promising a fortune in short-term
        leave available any and every for all-hours
        delivery, skirting touchstones missed while lifted,
        squinting at the flood of sputtering lamps
        burning soundly

down, in the chasm
again/until the vices evict as tough-love guardians would, hearing
a hallway march, over-practicing on a business model suite
recorded backwards from a bell of repeatings muted in
        the clangor—
        shrill amalgam relief map detouring designs
        outlined in the yonder purlieus, showing
        cunning open-floor plans, wish-watching
        the unsolicited arrive prepared to entertain
        undressed in gracious defense of bad intentions,
        genetically attracted to their own catty likenesses
        but also swept away with unfamiliarity,
        suspicious of the impulse to be themselves in rule
        agreement and advancement of naturally sideways descent,
        because the money's running out and a front's moving in
        carelessly, replacing whereas with what-for, when
        there's just so much

unfinished business:

STORAGE

She smelled that cabin smoke again for a moment
while recovering a wool shirt boxed in the attic,
recollecting:

      the neighbor's dog with one blue eye patrolling
      stacked green wood
      bought with broken trust,

      the cold lights dancing with the trees
      creaking above burial mounds,
      too late to be glowworms,

      overgrowth hinting a path leading to impassable brush
      long abandoned by the crosscut
      hanging in that slatted shed,

      pacing the bitter floor early waiting for a woodstove
      awakening, creosote
      seasoning the flue,

      drying wash draped over the single high-back
      left from other furnishings
      sold to feed the rent,

      driving unsettled behind the wheel watching
      the gas gauge decline to a noontide stint
      where tankers waited for relief,

      shaken by discussions that would have to be taken
      out to the sidewalk beneath the tavern sign
      when he just
                would
                  not
                    leave.

The scent has somehow kept, unworn in retainment
until now; the trappings of deep winter,
dried from a wet cord.

TAD'S

it wasn't the last place and time
you chewed staring beyond
the wallpaper flocked with discharged cook-toughs
honoring the medium-rare
just sliding down-in cafeteria soliloquy
discounted with silk tie hedges

off the square from a daily/weekly
stairway landing of plywood-doored hallways
lining the interior monochrome
tower walls with silent transients
passing above
the plexiglass lobby payphone

sending the message from that death-gazing progenitor
upset by the confrontational display of his own failings
seeming suddenly fragile
in false-positive reminiscence
as a bastard of a shunned bride
miscarried by late-recall

night-visits of an open-robed dandy
continuing enabling returns with a ticket back
offering to bear the weight of demise
listing manically
uneven in the procession
refusing to try

in the shoes of a frozen odometer sedan
departed slipping on
the rumored fruit of an auctioneer's pool
pocked-decking wife
giggling a soft brook of frosted flip invitation
leaving you cherry-toed for life and later

turning down your gated bartending
preparing for a dirge sung by a child
sent to holy rollers

frying their custodial pass-around
until the next reunion arranged in time
for bible camp refugee baptismal garb

revealing a born-again member
clinging beneath in wet translucence
for the laying-on of hands up chubby thighs
under the latchkey activity table
while choking down juicy gospel
across the county road

from a mobile-classroom sacrament
committed at a hog kennel dog attack
where spread-legged FFA wranglers
squirming stoic in the mud
held the squealers as guts spilled out over the levee
from a vinyl purse widow sitting for a sunrise

transported mistakenly risen
from nowhere else to go outside
the cabinet loyally cut by a laboring bleeder
smiling to pass the coffee can honesty test
that caught you shamefully gathering but never breaking
in your struggle from ongoing separations

jacking the sunken foundation
below a shocking first climax
confirmation from the closeted upper shelf
secret readings only an address down
from a foreign exchange waif watching a loose mutt
host a daylight free-for-all

ending under the covers
littered in a slime of other predictions
wholly manifested from natures on safari
led by an oath to cut the bloodline off
where it served you cheap and crawling
right down to the bone of then-but-still

The Funeral Years

The funeral years are here,
surging as distant warnings wail
incognizant to the silenced who carry on
losing track on the trail of unearthed damage,
left incomplete only as tilted monuments
misplaced along the open-grave furrows
carved by their own contesting hand
clawing at what they still cannot grasp,
too believable to accept

       (beginning bundled
       in a few early violent exits by exiled kin
       bowing near the oven or fuming from the garage:
       their shapes burned into silhouette
       by the ever-dimming who pass,
       themselves merely myths
       whispering their truths;
       shared passages, lit with disowned illumination,
       failing to connect)

          aftermaths starving
          for whatever yesterday will digest
          while collecting at the carving board

to be cut pirouetting
in the blades of yellowing grass
bitterly swaying dry with lost sensation,
neither still-young nor worn beyond use,
born succumbing as they pace their time
in place of rest already tired
from obligated favors interred with regifted aggression
or passive abandon let to force a way
to wherever it will penetrate. Hope is an opiate

(-expectation fleeing its abusers' wonts,
deranged with denial,
fumbling in the feeding line,
slavering along, plated
with petty wrap-ups of fragranced insinuations
scolding self-made characters; specters interrupted
by the surprise of their own evanescence,
revolving on the pyre spit
listening for suggestive redactions)

> excusing any related accusations,
> unnamed while dropping in,
> mispronounced at the wake.

Apparently

Is it what it is?,
summoned by the lofty
while staked amongst the grounded dregs
who anxiously pick at the evidence of waiting
in lost containment,

> looking for something
> that, still, just isn't
> there from a failure to process

> what misused reigns squandered
> in adventure, obeying the pledge
> of ruined rule,

> swallowing what has to be
> swallowed in order to swallow something else
> hearing neutral harbingers lying out of spite.

This *is* it!,
when the vacant lot is full of itself,
peddling a floodplain to meltdowns serving back
pocket vodka with a beef stick bar swizzle to an outskirts-type
who began by quitting

> everything, one thing at a time,
> eventually quitting even that too,
> living without the damnation of a heaven;

> a resinous drifter teased and left
> crying in the dusty ejaculate of moving on
> to never, forgetting how to beat the overblown

> home to the wrecking grounds,
> self-incarcerated, drinking for a mark
> left from broken rules minced oath-deep in taboo.

(And, all the while,
no one speaks
about *it*. All
conversations veer
around *it*
like rattling beaters
weaving over
roadkill; pressing-on
with the residue
spray fading
into low demand.)

Forecasts announce
clear skies as sleet begins to fall
but the pundits only report "well, clouds *will* be clouds…"
suspending judgment from folded arms,
ever-suspect

in the latest of serial fair-weather offers,
plowing through, despite all of history and basic science,
across the tangled maze.

Halos flare as a crow screams and circles
above, pleading for rescue
after an unending winter of eating its own;

ashamed of the act committed by concession,
but continuing out of survival.
And, never satisfied. Apparently.

Still

first seen as a shadow still
hanging, with no introduction
defined as a warning shot,
displayed with driven exposure
taken from the initial instant,
reaching from an image, then
so-to-be, moving as it was,

inconvertible from an inner state
umbilical grapevine divider,
probably smiling into the wind,
high on abandoned will and free to give
breath with the taste of a little death
on the way, in a green husk orchard
dropping late

> down unarmed hills with hands above the wheel,
> challenging luck won back in the defaulting night
> -walks to stair lamps smoldering with returning
> rush to a left-opened door

> leading deeply inside to young secrets embraced
> beyond the edges meeting at their peak above
> a window of elders witnessing failing prophecy
> dramatically pushed into confessions

> > made, *Broken*,
> > coldly taken,
> > selfishly saved;
> > *Stolen*, yet

trying with interning mentors' concerns
unveiled with careful alarm, quietly
waking the relentless lightning
stricken with its very sky pulling away
as not to fall, onward in the blur
of fleeting summer heat, locked out
with past-belongings

somehow never missing, behind
a vanishing point once shared
in rooms of last resort, offers
best-withdrawn and addressed
with the patience of a lost invitation
sent in light of the same darkness
as pictured, but without that shadow, since

This was not expected

in the waking dream shimmer of lost settlement lights
sensed miles away, aglow for the aging hours,
teasing as you continually breached
       summits in switchbacks. So, what
       did your hairpin-fragile guardrails forbid
       as even a chance to glance
          forward in relief?:
              An ascension
              reassessed

in the thrust over your limits to find only more distance
waiting in withdrawal, called from beyond longing
out of rejected nostalgia
       for times you weren't so clear. Yet, blind
       acceptance from others also only on the prowl
       for misleading destinations earned
          which perceived reward?:
              A phosphene
              vision rising

in the confusion of a final journey, approaching
radiance shared stirring near a threshold-withheld
arms'-length-anyhow always-there-assumed,
       somewhere returned sustained. But, traveling
       further still by simply staying behind,
       the sky is here to nearly save you
          now with this?:
              This was
              not expected.

INDEPENDENCE

Last year,
doors locked in liberty,
it was a crawl to destiny across dust and dander
racing to the bowels of a disloyal promised-realm
manifesting a carved memorial of twisted composure
as a mob condescended along a discarded vein
banking on a releasing delivery of relevance.

Or the year before,
off in the sketchy patchwork,
walking down a minor-league main street, lost
under a confectionary moon of hit parade pigment-terror,
a sweet-rot death-scent breeze surrendered
bleacher lookouts and flag runts saluting the qualified,
on territorial holiday, full sleeved under the heat.

Or the year before that,
pried from the cage
ajar to a sloping mezzanine, upon hearing the high
rumblings of allegiance, the carriers buckled,
leaving a sprawling shape breathing heavily
dismounted on a warped landing as the colors splayed
above to rouged howls of delirious victory.

Or go forth,
birthright still-born of belaboring faith
preying to save the alighted evening wasted counting
the fireflies of July, and instead inhale the musty
explosions inherited in failure as charred blossoms
mistaken in remembrance and seeded in the homelandfill
composting but never turned

      over in timeless celebration,

         lapsing from the shadows

            rooting through forever,

              for y'all

                  in dependence.

Premeditation

back Then,

but only occasionally,
dreamt high from a stronghold between
closed doors proffering warm lies in smiling retreat,
stretching out with open hands and locked eyes,
singing psalms of fruition across the battle line
      from incensed cold-earth tributaries
              rising from immeasurable depths,
        churning and praising subterranean channels,
            admitting living martyrs
      stripped of their stone ships flagged with veils
            of empathic masks, obsolete in the dark,
                revealing what is only
                revelation-extinguished origin
                    held together
                    with disconnected threads,
            refusing to be forgotten,
        warring wars-to-be.
      Time comes when
the ticking stops,

as Man,

gathering shards, dispersing
panicked silence, torture-worthy enough
to break reasonably upon returning heroic in-the-making,
though the spine can't tell which way is forward
or at least won't say,
      drunk with wandering free will,
           only pondering how long it can stay
      leaning, smoking bent halfies in an alley doorway,
           exhaling the past below one closed eyelid
      spasming above pouting plans eroding as they chafe

cracked lips of swollen-tongue-spit
rulings babbled blindly,
as a fat hand in a child's glove
pawing at the air,
mewling misunderstood
demands, only guessing
which way fantasized
towers fall
in, refuting premeditation

Assaulted while on a med run

by necropolitan free-timers
stiff from marriage-money junk
in a small town on the mend
trying to get a leg up on its fluid
migration, high enough to charm-from
at sidewalk cafe tables
flush with means—

       Where there is no one, except the leased
       handouts who are, at most, fears that
       creep past

in a claimed book shoppe
souveniring unabsorbed tomes
watered-down into dry cliché
by the deep-throating rote
who keep them expensive,
sold on/out
of context—

       Where quaint caricatures only exist famously
       condensed and served family style,
       grazing

on spitballed genres
dodged with no apologies
chewing off gummie-adult
activity lists to color-in
the time of spawn-pawns
trending out-of-stock,
consuming unfocused—

       Where blooming animals are trapped
       by a kill shot of continual,
       trivial disappointment

in thrift boutiques
reselling false memories
to breathy hagglers slouching over
trinket displays of polished knobs
repurposed out of respect
to chicken-bone-ivory
bistro teams—

      Where the allowanced wallow,
      soaked in idle-schedule
      lunches, spatting and sipping

on scented caffeine tinctures
over-presented at any rate,
merely picnicking with the sours
out of charity-duty
cemetery baskets of country-living
buzzing with the decent weekend
insurgency of estate—

      Where there is nothing of note that is at-least,
      handed down from atmospheres of decay
      passed-on painlessly playful

            by necropolitan
            free-timers
            stiff from marriage
            -money
            junk
            in a small town
            on the mend.

in completion,

you are where you are
when the work has done nothing
but endure, as you finish off at last
with an emission of cold ideals
calling like jackals whimpering
at your growing distance,
lost in the search

from the horror of incompletion:
words merely failing
where you meant they should,
glaringly buried in cryptic speech
hushed by disaffirming offers
scrawled in obscured judgments
that you fall for every time

no one can be trusted;
especially you, now
when the truth turns away
too totaled to get a sober rise
beneath the desire to be left
alone, clinging to your fable
at stake in such barren fields,

cropped out impartially
framed by a hostile bedside light
just showing off
to the discontinued past
what senseless dreams allow
back when it's strolling in late
rain check-waiting room disrepair,

treasonous with meaning
abbreviated 'til you've gone
where everything else stops
working at once, realizing
there is no horizon,
: as dawn & twilight
are just exes that still fuck

in completion,
where you are;
where you are,
in complete
incompletion; you are,
where you are
incomplete

CIRCUMFERENCE of a SINKHOLE

Teetering at the edge of the cavity;
looking over with a torch,

you crawl out of a last call you won't remember slurring through
on a shell-buzzing morning
to the first floor of a closed lodge,
waiting for something to begin or end
at a table-window view of a frozen confluence,
where it bulges like a still-panting mouse,
alive and resigned to its fate, in the belly of a sleeping snake.

Upstairs, the doors are open
to aged but able-squeaking beds
covered in cold quilts.

You can pick any room you like;
no one else will be checking in.

Dropping slowly,
the bottom must be coming.
Above,
the light is now just a pinhole

you arc with barely time for a few miniatures,
turning in your seat to flag down a wet bar attendant,
only to land warm but dry and walk
out into the open-legged night
looking for a tossed pillow to holler into
until you can think upright
to lie your way, all the way back.

Awakening at the ledge,
on a trail tracing the rim
where either direction is fine
or not-fine but final,
gusting on the lip

you blow past for a stripdown with an inspector
whose eyes pop like there's never been such a mess
-collection of reckless exit punctures
and may even be impressed
by your commitment to abandon the indelible evidence
linking continents with skin to drift in,
baking then stinging at a crunchy pub colony
slammer, in a shower of loose-attention lunch pints,
sweating on the way to a matinee dance bed
slithering out of instincts the beers find funny
but a complimentary choreographer doesn't
before you can sleep it off and slip out
in a missing ride that swings you to a tarmac gate
with room enough to atrophy

    onward through the entombment

you drive-on to an economy class mid-day reserve
stocked with a feral fawn
freely buttering up and cutting its own rug
surrounded by barbeque hustlers,
beer pimps and a double-fisted gulper
who lectures specifically about nothing,
listing with a strand of shredded meat swaying
like a dashboard hula figurine
hanging from a juiced bag under one of his red eyes.

You don't mention it.

He finishes his dissertation and moves on
to another opinion-prisoner.

Zigzagging in other interruptions
an hour later, you see the guy again;
he still has the garnish.
No one has told him:
maybe because they couldn't get in a comma of exodus

or because, like you,
they found the pendent shred more intriguing
than the word-clouds burping from his tap
into the open-pit dusk.

Turning at the mouth,
tasteless and drooling,

you narrow from the infinite to the isolating,
penetrating canyons to over-confident summits
on-holiday gliding into the flat lap of ag,
charred tips and late-night hammered re-hash
saints screwing in lieu of arch dessert, parked
in diner lot cars fogged by charm forgotten
after visiting tables of borrowed strangers
staggering to spa in blue-feathered Easter hats
en route from death trip cities dotted along
windy lakes off cheese curd byways.

A section of the path falls
into the darkness

you roll-in, to a train station lounge, loading off the rails
with a ripped pair of empty nest tourist mommies
showing souvenir snaps of trees budding
goats and cheering tumblers
near a stumbling crag who leafs through his passport
to prove that he isn't someone you've heard-of
at a street brawl opening act
rocking a reprimand in a foreign tongue
kiss-off from a transplanted cactus
with nothing riding, always clinging.

On the brink of climbing
out to continue the unnatural
nature walk,

you blink once to find yourself
squinting from morning light,
sleepwalking through familiar drills
practiced like the real thing,
separating with a bomb scare ultimatum,
as final as the night triggered to abandon everything
with the dawning last throw in defeat
of mistakenly disposable dreams left behind
a transit dumpster breaking free
north of north, turning and burning,
armed with possessions slowly expedited,
diminished as stars crawling on their knees,
shooting back from another temporary citadel

    longing with secrecy.

You hobble for wine and muscle relaxers
after bowing down easily in a rebounding pinch
to pet a rough angel's pooch, moaning as you hug
onto a haunt until rendezvousing
with that pardoned almighty
example, pulling castrated roots
towards attempted rebirth
through dry county benders called home,
placing memories into dusty storage
before moving on in a land-grab
heritage cab tipping off its favorite places to hate,
letting you out at a divot
left in the green of a motor court cabin
to recite a broadside penned in forearmed confusion
to paralyzed witnesses,
losing enough for a free casino key
while old men bat blind drunk
canes at each other's hungover groins
sliding trays in the buffet line
as you straddle between first and third wheel,
hinting a menu of popular infections
to a hypochondriac, out of justifiable offense.

Dusty jets of groundwater mist
lose their will and fall wherever

you end up, met with reminders of lost relation,
in black-inked nails, fingerpainting
a warding symbol on the toe of only one shoe,
leaving the other scuffed
for cherished missteps still kicking back
while searching for other tiaras to discard,
now unable to tell rain from tears
staining the conclusive reality waiting within
the requested papers of release,

> *continuing towards the unmarked*
> *endpoint of the radius,*
> *wondering if the path is just*
> *the spine of an ouroboros;*
> *its shadow growing*
> *from your relentless flame.*

SLAKE

he'd swallowed her youth
in sips so small she wouldn't notice
until it was eventually
just remembered on dark afternoons

spent loosely settled
when the bet was whetted
with an unrequited ante
       ending
       in beginnings
       of everything,

between anywhere she could go
as-he-pleased, like they'd always been:
locked to the past in one-way
turnstiles only ushering them along,

letting things pass
after watching them come,
grabbing, in excused patterns,
       still seen when dryly looking back
       to neither turning around,
       surviving on habits

ravenous from nothing left to leave
but another bottomless impression
with a pickup-shift bartender asking
"Aren't you one of our daytime regulars?"

and she nodding a No,
silently adding: "but for now,
bring me my usual and then leave me alone
       with the running tab as evidence of my journey",
       tipping back with the tumbler,
       letting his ice hit her teeth

GHOST PARADE

The street was empty   *and you were alone,*
so you waited together;   *each, just*
stalled witnesses   *of nothing new*
     when they came down the middle:

     daylight drunks,
     young enough to be excused
     or sufficiently old for an allowance
     to reenact what they fondly missed,

     leaning on foot,
     pedaling on display
     or crashing their carriages into barricades,
     as they crushed in

     dressed-down
     like main drag flags,
     hanging from poles and shoulders,
     touched in colors of ashen preoccupation

     joined by the permanently-impaired
     striking off individually,
     uniformed as they were born,
     strategically bumming spares

     from the rolling influx, rounding up
     to be cleansed of their conceptions,
     pushing back from the little space
     they demanded was rightly reserved;

     warily tolerating
     each other's proud deliria
     enough to crawl in short excuse
     for a timeless incurable cause

of-coursing in formation,
insurgent and thrilled
with their own parade,
celebrating life

at home without
their lives in repeated sin
of coupled ends to a T
in said-town,

oh, the state
these things so-named
after an instinctual attraction
dedicated to their casual downfall.

The silence was terrifying;   *the spectacle, deafening*
as the emptiness continued   *to grow, too late now,*
when the street wandered off   *just before you did,*
both, speechless but not surprised.

Rest

Easy now:
night is back and you are one
under the cover of darkness
where edgy utopiates
thrash with blind movement
under a black frost within
with nowhere still-there to go to.

So as they are, so are you,
from unpainted corner to exposed rafter,
paid on a running meter of silent subtraction
absurdly searching for counterpoints
climbing from beneath, enclosed upon,
hangin' in their beyond, with

stretched claws, sleep-twitching
in a dream-romp comfortably curled up

your interior
hourglass of peace,
reclining ergo static
between thinly cut scraps
layered unevenly, weighted
by the design of solitude
while a sky of raining glass
cries a slurry of its own,
groaning for a return
to the gutters

when commerce punches out early
to grab a bite and then maybe get laid

before the alarm clock rings-in
morning's interrogation,
lightly searching your fretting folds
for signs of weakness
or hastily made plans
abandoned ahead,

deep in the revving drift
defining the margins of the dead trunks
leaning bare-assed in uprooted exposure,
bowing to welcome you along,
as blood and breath need each
for either other to continue,
                                        to rest-easy now:
night is back and you are, too.

Fumes

A breezy rain catching
the heat in a lucid haze,
focusing indeterminate

steam or smoke
rising with early morning
weather pressing

on a mossy shingle roof,
silently alarms you
enough to climb an interior

flight to what is neither
wall nor low ceiling
forming your upper limit;

palms held flat
against the indecisive
garret angles feel

the relief of coolness
sealed in the mystery
just beyond the frame.

However, within
a closed-windows stream
allowing intruding

daylight to travel
above the groaning
streets and rustling yards,

either a fog obscures
your vision or a wraith
appears to be

opaque with clear allusion:
you're the misty vapor
of your own exhaustive fumes.

GET-TOGETHER

When no one is going anywhere, all of us are dreaming

whatever we can
        in the slack-hour'd days' decisions made-up for grabs
        reaching back for nearly anything but the end,
        concluding it's too early yet to pore over,
            iced with memory
            salted to go down faster;
            dry tongues longing for more
                than they can afford but somehow do
                to put a face on the morning
                they've been left with;

            all of this,

backing up to search around for what's missing

in the moments
        lost to merciful exchanges with estranged reminders
        showing up unannounced, offering empty arms,
        suddenly there just to *get together*,
            thirsty for an eternity that can be lived now,
            while it can still be
            tasted, though the daylight is wasted
                again, modeling as night,
                pointlessly posing
                its inferred query,

            (asking) as if to state:

(*Don't you*)

        worry about others
        trapped in the circle
        they've made of themselves: you

(want to)

have what they can't
know; what they don't
miss yet somehow still

(enjoy);

that what's always been: nearly,
elsewhere you don't know,
when who you were, simply, questions

(how you are.)

since no one is going anywhere, but all of us are dreaming.

Chatterbox

(a knuckle tap on a closed door)

Hello?
Sorry to bother you, but, well,
your past has arrived
ahead of time,
asking where you've been.

I said you were away
but it pressed me,
so I told it you *may* be here,
but in the dark
…upstairs, I said pointing to my temple,
removing your shoes and pacing quietly,
probably pulling at your ole soft spot,
chewing on your lip
and turning around after you'd hit a wall.
…*usually*, I meant to say,
…turning
…*or* hitting a wall.

Either or neither, I guess.

Right?

Then, I said it could also be that you were packing
…or maybe even still *un*packing
…or

It cut me off
and asked when it could see you;
that it thought it was expected.
I joked that *both* of you have probably been waiting
for this; for the other
to come forward.

It smiled.
…I *think* it was a smile, anyway.

And, oh yeah, it offered a gift bag.
I looked inside: mostly final notices
and form letters of intent;
in your style,
but unsigned.
Some, torn into confetti.

It also said it composed an appendix
to include, but didn't;
said it didn't want to quote
unquote *spoil the ending*.
But, I have that as well,
nicely folded
as a chatterbox.

At first, I found this taunting,
but now I find it kind.

So, I'll just leave it all here,
outside your door.

It said it'll return again though.

I only knocked when I heard
what I thought
was a shoe drop,
…or a shot.

Hello?

as one

      in scant rant admission
of dayspring deranged by time-honored decline,
the traffic slows our enhanced estimates into detainees
stalled in fragile deadlock dread, lived-in-waiting;
light relief letup off ramps passed in lost musings,
hummed and thumbed on a war-drum steering wheel
in the throes of seizing glows that enflame the uneasy,
easily captured, accepting the challenging limits
expanding in the unknown glory hinted at by those
sedated supernovas whispering
            "be strong, but not *too*…"

      …viable; thruways retracing
the last melting mirrors staring back and zoning
off in single-serve committees, departing precooked
on concrete plans in the congestion breathing slowly
out, past self-led examination found wistfully
looping with daymares on the lam, abridged, only
shrieking what they've been told, then reading-on
in soaked landslides, unsettling, on their own way down
from a naively active fault, traced to a beast-made human
nature, thus inclined, speeding into a bottleneck
      rising broken on a popular road

            pressed to lips hushing with pleasure,
                bled from vacant valves
          spouting flat-out truths
              elated on the weighted loads
          dispersing excuses to boilermakers
              insistent on half-full resignation
          next to that *That*:
                sportsmanlike *Like*,
                supposed victor:
                only/coldly winning;

so touching, so lasting, so-fukn-what;
    outcomes are mere instances
fingered in tarnished luster
    slobbering in the cheers
listening to what cannot be
    accurately worded flare-ups
inwardly shooting skyward, pissing
    over the drifters
    left in hoed rows
    leading all the way

    to ornamentally-hooded registrars
preserved in monumental adherence and wheezing
as they weep *"mercy me!"* in late-discovered
constellations of near-relation, distantly reminiscing
with sucked-gut feelings, spit-fixed to dismiss in terms
not met nor negotiable with weak delivery, fulfilled
by their very failure: all napping ticks born to release
their toxic awakenings of closed imagination repurposed
then circulated in private potlucks no longer secreted
from hungering masses of ego gourmands in din-din bibs
    serving spells already entranced

    by their onanistic byline image,
crusting in honorable mention from groping for life's rewards
upon submission with a non-binding vow that says,
"Sure, I'm open to *paying* suggestions." sunglassed
to expose the enemy, seeing itself as the end that is already,
gullible to the flirtatious future, in trade or transference,
or ideal idea of being, lest undeserved,
overfeeding the screaming why-nots scribbling
out in panic as ambition emerges, charging forth,
kicking its ass between the eyes wincing in
    slo-mo sightseeing descent

    vacationing at the axis of excess discipline,
    in the sublime supine,

estranged to move freely
      amongst ever-shifting states of mania
in tie phenomenal withdrawal
      from a board-game, playing with its selves
of homegrown juniors in a lullaby-rage,
          cradled on the laps
          of predatory allies,
          gurgling repeated choruses

memorized by twin confederations,
      made-up and-of anthem-grunts
strutting in lockgoosestep-ball-change
      on self-ordained
celebration leashes,
      chain-caroling
"we sing to thee as versos/
      in recto ruination/
      for whom is of us either/
      enjoined, so shall we stay"

PASSING

a car wreck that lasted
half a century just trying to get out;
now to check the damage:

feeling there must be injuries,
unknown by being exactly everywhere;
possessions strewn across, of what's left

      within, the median-itself dismissing
      there could be anything separating
      different routes moving blindly

        past on either side, even

      while standing lost between,
      wondering which direction
      it was all going, fast

when everything started
spinning, or never left
and this is where it began,

eternal or external; unimportant
really, now facing the way
you've just always been

The Thinning Apex

like the old guy about Your age:

pacing the sidewalk outside the barbershop with the fly-down
meth-tic bar-belly and maybe-accidental collar-up

large-cell-talking about his upcoming court case and what
he heard-or-read-somewhere-can't-remember-now
about what *she'll* have to actually prove

scratching his other ear then looking at his short/fat digging finger
with squinched eyes and twisting mouth and wiping on his pants
before reinserting after lighting a smoke

as he explains what really didn't happen the way *she's* making it
sound

and a chair inside opens up

ahead of the couple born soon after Your last breakage:

who look like the smell of a tossed-off top-sheet discharge
amidst-summer late-morning beach rental lotion breeze

with her plucked brows and foundation stick spackling

and his plucked brow and skull spasming to a nineties cross-over
beat on an otherwise lifeless carcass, slumped while he stares
ahead, fixed on nothing

as she leans her head on his shoulder and lets a painted nail
wander-drag to the washed denim zipper fold while smirking
into his dead eyes

next to the mother younger than You by her teen's age:

waiting for her vacation-custody to shear his visitation locks

while she covers her happy-gasps under over-smiling eyes and
phone-snaps the temporary-reunion cleanup event

instead of whatever else is usually cheerfully paid-for and cut short
after mimosa-brunch tollway casino weekend stayovers messaged
in with snorting spurts excused by shifting obligations

       and the smoking defendant looks in and realizes
       he's missed his turn but keeps on attacking and
       lights another

       and the beach corpse explains to the stylist his
       side-fade-trim hopes & dreams as his zipper-nail
       takes her incoming call outside in a crop top
       pink-sweats swish

       and the shorn son stands with his mom-date
       running her fingers through his pared virgin
       mane and chirping what they should do with
       the rest of the day until he gets picked up and
       later she will too

but, it's Your turn now as the collar and bib engage:

to take off just enough to casually push the years back behind the
ears, aware that the thinning apex will appear when the clipping
ends and the chair is turned

with one mirror facing another, capturing what no one can see
on their own but shortly recognize from others revealed clearly
in Your true reflection,

Oh, 00

The naughty aughts' zeros

cancelled out, leveled by highs and lows that weren't;
just opposite endings of the same talus:

sloping below from an uppercut to a dropping jaw
decaying with loose libidos extracted while still grinding
easily on the greasy lap of impatient time

skulking within a spirit-blanched skeleton, avoidance-drinking
until stiff from surviving now-defunct in brief return
to an underground wintering lair that would later bear
knotted snakes grinning beneath the spawning floe of the coy

scrims of vernal light who summoned solstice beer bottles
to rise like empty lilies, emerging with the thaw,
fenced-in by snow-bandaged hedges
hiding clubbing bruisers stepping out
swinging still-curtained rods bent on oilfield poison

chased without proof or other diluting residual
remaining proposed in homewrecking repair, taking settlements
seduced by the payload, dazzling beyond the routine of drilling
down fully-vacant as an abandoned hotel haunted by the half-limp
proprietors of swerving conscience, weaving in and out
of crossed-line lanes as if either sewing or ripping a seam,

looking back at the fraying, now showing
it was neither and both crash-landing and left, hanging
fingertips to crossed ankles from opposing ceiling fan blades
spinning out in representative never-ending nihilistic pursuit,
claiming victim in a spree of buzzing one-offs

retching from low balconies of blasé disbelief, viewing
over-welcomed ass-diggers of avalanching moderation
allowed to roam openly, fielding theories
embraced to keep the mystery intact

on lost nights chugging along nowhere but in the way,
to somewhere-to-be, en route with free admission
looking for a final way out

for nothings who ought to say *when*, but won't,
or where or how to fall,

already lying side by side.

bound,

as everything slows in the lowering light, rising

over truck stop crushed-gravel bawling engine growls.

      : a woman yells *You're a whore!*

standing adjacent a passenger door-open pickup

idling at a holstered pump

with a man leaning back on the tailgate,

arms relaxed to thumb-hooked pockets,

gazing courteously away, appearing lost

in thought somewhere else

and waiting to go there

      , when, *It still hurts!*, phone to her ear,

held quietly for a moment now,

head down then suddenly skyward

as if in search for anything

attempting composure

with a relaxed *Okay.*

I love you.

I gotta get my stuff outta this man's truck.

; concluding with a hesitant finger-peck,

returning the borrowed cell to the man

reaching in the bed for a canvas tote

brightly colored beneath a darker peace sign collage,

parking the twisted strap onto her shoulder

while patrons drift across the c-store lot,

some turning to look and others pretending not-to,

under the graying pink bruise of approaching night

. the truck crunches-off to the frontage road,

sunset leaving just her silhouette sitting

at a cement picnic table to light a cigarette and rest

a tilted head on an elbow-propped hand, exhaling

spirals of either releasing or tethering strands,

Everyone is driven unknowingly to their urges,

going down arising
lost as a lone ice field
so gradually broken by
drops of rain merely being
who they are briefly within
a stark accumulation
betting they'll be numb
by the time they hit

casting shadows of kissing
darkness unconcerned
with gestures of comfort
in the last hours remaining
at terminuses lying desperately
exposed and unreachable
in plain view beneath
the mass watching

young hands release
the other sheared to collect
lighter with their own
but alive in the cold
devouring peace of nearing
spring that takes its time
seriously still as the season
mourns the fog of dawn

trailing the drawn-hustle market
journey to softly slip away
for a projection of dreams
spread to life from a small light
touching down with its story
filling emptied days
bothering in temptations found
distracting its vacant draw

never surrendering to the outpost
sending sweet elucidations
with the tough delivery
of a herder's cry
sirening alone to any
who turn unable to ignore
the passionate call
of unreturnable direction

pointing out the richness
born of dying lake bed
soil left to carry on
for reasons unknown
to the very nature made
from the gift of death
that stays living for anyone
who will listen close enough.

  To believe what you can't
when simplicity rules suddenly
one night with a sole answer
questioning what was never
accepted saving the intimate
allowance to run loose
along the shore with the tide
lapping from an ever-distant deep,

everyone is driven unknowingly to their urges.

for Eugene

(:)

religiously semi-(:)hallucinated on the throne
by a crowned vassal, royalty of the ordure chapeau.
    Prescribed in kraft accoutrement
as exploding bastions of scripture scullions
serving soiled tartlets of irrational fancy,

banquets of expression for the couponed-moral
expellees of shall-not, lazing in drugging hunger,
exceptional expectance and other loose reactions
exposed on the sublunary terrain of the vulnerable,
devoted to gorging on exhausted inspiration

coming suddenly in alarming fits, eternal
as fervor and decay composed in dual memoriam
majestic reward for the privileged
rumble from eruption to quietus
and its enlightening testament,

    the back-passage practice playing happy hour
low-range continued-in, character-dismissing
the demanded refund of artistic license
as result of a clean bill, in wasted repose,
without need to reexamine what wasn't found,

Y

to those ways known to hang on yet, not-yet
understood, before too-long-before
up ahead, somewhere must also be through,

since-transfixed
with still air motioning

to then,
gusting back the bangs
over watering
sunsetting eyes,
drying
exposed gums

facing the speed of a downhill past, launched
wide-legged and feet-away like a coasting
Y, as de/parting will also be staved

freely blurring
by without bystanders
initially between,
with no self
found in the rush
to the bottom

that maybe knows   what you didn't

while slowing from the impact
of a spill merely riding out a passage,
so-moving just-so, its stillness can't be stopped

under wheels left spinning on from never braking
until seemingly broken, asking the unspoken answer
Why *all* things withheld shouldn't also be released

Work

To wait,
sometimes in a room
but often in a car
after driving
to wait for something else,
you park and move to the passenger seat
and watch.
This *is* work,
sitting with the window down an inch,
triggered by whatever's going on,
recalling the details.:

> Times when there was no car to wait in
> or when you had a car but had no business being in it,
> > heading somewhere
> > for reasons that no longer matter
> > (or maybe didn't even *then*),
> > ending up somewhere without consequence
> > for the act of getting there
> > (places you shouldn't have gone)
> > but, bored or obsessed, you just haaaaad to
> > get out and stir something up.:
> Times when you didn't have to wait, but did,
> or when you should've waited but just couldn't

> > > hold it in

> > > > any longer,

> > > > > when the world was endless,

> > > > with places

> > > to wait.

At a used car dealership, recently,
the salesman wouldn't stop, going off,
"Listen, you seem like a reasonable guy…",
unaware of your work
reappraising
past decisions in renewable review,
demanded by the weight
of explanations that can't determine
what drove you elsewhere then,
now with nowhere left
to wait.

Unknown, but for the Animals We Could Be

Arriving as crashing strays of invited strangers,
watching from solitary stakeouts,
introduced scavenging
a half-bottled-BYO affair,
reforming mid-way as a single
stranger of two

failed magnets repelling
shavings with a carry-out stolen
            on a dare, down the street
                        leaning on a hood
                                    exchanging the basics,
                                                you said you knew

a place with an open invitation
to come-up-anytime *but soon because,*
your friend said, *well, you know….*

Slurring a dreamed hour spin,
awaking opposite sides of cornered
couches blanketed by our coats and momentarily
surprised by a DIY mountain
retreat-in-process driven-to on barely remembered
winding stretches along sheer drops to blackness

claiming occasional
impetuous swerves,
            an early-afternoon open door
                        to sunlit red clay pines chilled
                                    the room a silent man made
                                                with a woman

warmly recalling
the late unannounced arrival
with liquor shared until light.

Your friend left for her shift
and the man showed us around the property,
pointing a beer-canned-hand to bear markings
on trees and thumbnail
plans of exterior
repair in arrears.

We showed up as evening reached out,
where the woman worked and the man ordered
        while studying other men
                also ordering,
                      noting how they joked with her
                              and how often she smiled back

until his detouring
of dialogues dragging on
just too long.

                              Your friend had confided
                              he would come most
                              every shift, *imagining*
                              scenes later mumbled
                              out at home in accusing
                              monologues veering off
                              blurring observations

                              until passing out.
                              Unable to sleep,
                              she would listen
                              in the darkness
                              as *huffing* and *scratching*
                              circled outside
                              somewhere close….

Bodies sloshed into the gaps the bar refilled
as we designed a sudden goodbye to slip out

in the rush. When we rose, the woman looked
forsaken beyond the taps. The man continued
swilling in surveillance, waving a see-ya-around
without turning from his watch.

And we navigated downward,
curving back into the valley
     where we began, returning
         as we left, to remain strangers
             dropping off after colliding,
                then moving on easily;

unknown,
but for the animals
we could be.

Free

From that first ash: in easy decline

> splitting for the rails,
> buzzing in the heat

> tracking and expanding,
> static on their way;

> in no shape or need then
> for anything, less whatever

> turned so early, slowly killing
> off what would come

for whoever all that led to,

> dizzy in the aftermaths
> of difficult escapes.

To that last cut: in tough growth

> boiling with the colleagues'
> probables of *nothing*

> burning in near-guesses,
> promising *we'll see*;

> feeling there might be
> more time for whenever,

> to heel from the late force
> of recovery, still swollen

for being whoever you're from,

> sutured with new endings
> just beginning to be free.

Yield

anywhere the lit image leers,
either sequestered in the unsparing air
panting to catch a breath high above the water
or laid bare at the expanse where it splits, blinking
as if crying on the surface to an interior mystery

roiling below, both staring back prescient but silent,
the way even a grown child knows what-was,
yet unable to question how while continuing on
innocently, reliving the emptiness of pressure
that fills every unnoticed cavity,

subtly gnawing deep in the bone, at first far away,
sighing an approaching universe of rage
like a lost pin waiting, hidden to be stepped on
in the night, or head-on lights seen only when upon,
too sudden for a screaming surprise

late-recollection of ignored warnings
discarded with the zero-hour tocsin,
revealed as a delayed plea from the endless
harmonic-turned-coda rising darkly away,
strong with unstoppable reckoning,

cold, as pulse realizing instantly that it isn't
what it could've been, up to that last moment,
now, when our briefness is our definition,
whole, w/o those 1/2-guessed intros
skipped one prelude at a beat,

adding and diminishing with each lurid step
mistaken as a stride storming off
with unrecorded time-served to keep the minutes'
other hand slowly feeling up the runaway seconds
left in as linear proposals-to-be,

murmuring curt regards never recognized as a smirk
from the undercurrent, knowing the breakers are clever
tears of anguish streaking down our cheeks—
and so, by finishing that last drink then making another
or swallowing the pill by taking the rest,

unanswered responses redress all questions
demanding *tell me what you see*,
while standing on the shore unsure if you're watching
the moon or its reflection on the waves
laughing as they crash, licking at the senses

unconsciously conjured and impossibly embraced,
when you swim out to be found
cresting with the spume swelling in the trough,
neither giving nor relinquishing, you simply yield
anywhere that lit image leers.

Offering

what you know you don't know
standing between arbiters
clinging to each other in mutinous
defense, guaranteed to entertain within

what is soberly sensed milieu
by the condemned Offering
conceived in surrendered mystery,
exhausted from accusations left within

what staggering legacy sees staring
back from a speculum of long-dueling loyalty
to morning-afters of sole-after-sole blackout-lit
acceptance, confirmed invisibly-constant within:

high

on a romantic flight of longing,
maneuvering loose and low to cellars
speaking-easy in spiked rounds,

challenging alley cats to short cuts,
waking gold-laméd on sidestreets
betrothed but betrayed outside

an unfastened distance, returning coldly
stunned from the shouldered overall blur
rattling along the bars encircling the façade

dismantled from an extraction-fenced vista
fist of pulled-hair in biting décor bruisings
cancerous with grilled neighbors, alarmed

      one grounding night
            as a broken plume
            froze in its reflection
            mirrored as a blade
            suspended aloft over
            the throat of a cross
            headwind fighting to stay
            nested in the flocking
    from infidelities amassed

throughout the eloping drawn-line vows
unbound in ageless passion encaged
predestined in the pinion of young desire

STATION

The summits keep watch from intoxicated heights,
peering down on interred states tightly unassembled
       in chained-door rooms, sitting static merely sputtering
       hope in last-gasped sparks like downed power lines
       convulsing between the passing terrors

on passages of twister-carvings snaking over shaky country
exposing roadside crusaders threatening higher ground
       with a parochial compassion, invading then exonerating
       in stunted bandwidths of merciful enchantment,
       when & where the grids shudder,

              bolting from the tater patch
              loaded, base and somewhat
                  free, searching

the strata slits above, mulling over unsupported credo
cants of talk radio religionists dramatically advertising
       homespun 'blesid suggestions of last-days-again
       calling in their two cents after having a few-too-many
       & movin' on with *"I'm no scholar, but I'll be damned…"*

how much might-a-been missed only chasing dead air
particulates breezing from the overlook dreamt at a turnout,
       zoning in the comfort of worldly obsessions, beyond
       judgment, braking as they're passed mistakenly
       as just another bluff promising better inclinations.

TURNBUCKLE

Resorting to bed down swinging in a lost meadow
awakened in a lobotomized desert temple,
picked for a getaway with a drifting mirage
unrapt in a casino boxing match,

blend in with a blue velour jogging suit and gold chain
anchored with a large bejeweled dragon to hang over your death
metal tour T in a seat behind the ring announcer sporting
a pompadour wigging out in a tantrum.

The bell clangs:
      Home-remote bouts are distant & sterile visuals
      that pair well with apathetic between-rounds fridge-trips,
      but a few actual rows away you can smell emotion,
      humid in the pheromonal ether, thick in controlled panic

      and desperate recovery radiating from the fighters'
      wet faces flickering under the battle lights, reaching out
      to bring the upsetting question to an end, waited-for
      and watched as much as the engaging habitat landscape

      of coif turfs and tuck-n-roll cocktail jalopies grabbing
      around and over, hands gesturing and clutching currency,
      heads twisting quickly like monsoon weathervanes with
      torsos almost-rising, indecisive between seated bounces.
And then, it's suddenly over.

The crowd scatters out like lost moths
in jagged search for any new illuminations,
flitting to the lobby and spreading into the rabble porridge
bubbling with hot anxiety-air and chatter-shrapnel din,

clearing the way for other conclusions, struggling
on the quiet drive out that can't believe where it's going,
with nothing left to give, so taken with the blows, in a corner
where shown-ropes turn to continue, bound in tension.

FAULTY

swearing off the memories replaying uncertain scenes
as they're scratched into scars needing to heal,

heeling to needs stricken by the record,

    echoing the shallowness of offenses overheard
    recently needling the circumstances
        maintaining
            what can't be erased-in

                relying on their lines
                of wounded reasoning,

                dying to get carried away
                without drawing fault

buried in recollection, where the past is de facto
fiction pissed onto springtime snow banked over details

left beneath the ongoing unforgotten fallout, until now,

    turning up to be recited again, in recovery,
    with omissions remembered precisely
        as though
            they never even happened

Behind

The gaze that could bleed The light
was a limb That continues to grasp
At the throat of the gift,
Placed at the feet Or thrown to the step,

But left from the lips That didn't speak
up Over the cry Heard on a path
Picked to destroy The very one brought
To bring back a life Wrapped in a sheet:

      Stars on the skin,
      Fading from bad Incisions of choice,
      Were hidden or culled Parcels of time,
      Lulling back years That passed into sleep.

But, that's how it gets
At the tip of a knife Just piercing through
Those you can't know, Born out of loss,
And no shock to the prize No one will claim:

      Lower your voice
      And lay down your head;
      From where you are now,
      It'll come from behind.

Cuttings from the Tangle

INFLECTION:
the thicket between subtle
inference and stealthy intention
standing silently-being
mere stresses spit out
smooth as grits piecemeal-sporked
with a margarine nipple melting
to mask the coarse-grain bite

of bunched bines
       fancied in continual-light deprivation
       as conifer boles cut clean-as-can-be,
       slivering their own nails,
       smitten with toothless blades
       just going down again on warped planks
       weakened at the macula knots
       self-described as "beauty marks",
       metastasized and spreading
       in private dysplasias
       clubbing at poolside group-interview
       mixers on legal hunt holiday

       just a-soakin' in their genesis,
       "okay, fine" with a severance
       radiation of mores pulsing under
       the superficial warmth of a former star
       flaring at will with savage licks
       cast to a vast spinning-barrel sky
       so apparent that it just cain't be,
       seen-though/believed-in, so therefore
nuthin-much can be done-such without

RECREATION:
a chain of mimicking chains
pulled in defeated repeats
as a pastime seasonal,

rubbed raw and smoked
in a soothing worship
salve or other timeless balm
bombs with pom-poms

bearing cones
casually dressed-up in distress flags
tortured by and large for truth,
popularity or other sports
captured in a stroking tension
wind-driven wild
while erect at half-mast,
hindgut-choking on sugar

-coma'd tornados of reduced-cream risen;
swirling unicorn shit horns
sighing a pinched-tip
saliva string of heritage
clinging to traditional trappings
snapping back as they shun

PROGRESS:
removable headway dressed
in a loose, decorative
bandage serving the wound
at the pleasure of the infection

from needle-leaf branches
enwreathed in a hoedown,
frisking around a bonfire
sizzling with enkindled id,
en masse at sponsored history gatherings
readdressed with updated backstories,

praying in uniform
loose-association to branded tired-tread
spike strippers flat-faced on the red carpet
pulled at a locked-exit gala

by a tour-wand-winded narrator warning
"just take your drink ticket and move along"
in quiet disagreement to the farthest edges
touched by mirror balls hanging
off-the-hook in done-deal reach-around

SUSPENSION:
on display in exclusion,
from a shear laterally-shifting
literal shafting

gentlemen's-handshake allegiance-grip
sac-deep in u-turning paternalist habits,
in a tussle over an intervention re-do
with open bar reception following
in practical cavalcade,
slipping on nut-shelled quick-fix orations

misheard from ez biddings wafting
from a midway auction yard speaker
raffling off a mystery dinner barn event
postponed to accommodate a host of rascals
milling past remotely,
opening with a disclaimer,
jumping over each other to push the point
away from home and never get out
satisfied with a thing
but a stun gun trained on the tenderloin,
so-called-for but acceptable with a moderate

TOLERATION:
the kind-alike sacrifice
endowed to enforce
given-permission publicly,
until inconvenient
or less cost-effective
in private like-kinds

within and around
　　　　voluntarily crumbling ramparts; repurposed
　　　　under-crust dams of pie-eyed swollen meat
　　　　bartering self for gristle that-is;
　　　　that is, swallowed scrapings,
　　　　cud-chum slinger fed-swung
　　　　directly at the penned and growling
　　　　fodder-they

　　　　cringing beyond a towne square
　　　　stained window reflection,
　　　　flashing gas-lit illuminations
　　　　bellowing within imagination,
　　　　shattered behind shuttered dreams
　　　　eroding as they wake
　　　　"just goin' about our business", adjourned
　　　　early with a pinned spray of thorny sprigs
　　　　pruned for wounding their shady neighbors
　　　　freshly mangled in the lede by the ruminant,
　　　　throwing down the mittens and cocktailing
　　　　behind protective-anger party masks,
sensationally inducing

ELISION:
married by omission
with the flip of a weighted coin
spinning for the spoils,
gestured in code

-enhanced concentrations
　　　　czar'd by temp assistant-camp-managers
　　　　stationed at the tribal margins
　　　　on promotional lockdown special
　　　　offered with feverish immunity,
　　　　qualified by the very icy-dicey
　　　　nature of control, just upgrading-through
　　　　with natural conviction,
　　　　striking curled knuckles clasping

corners of mesh-enclosure safety-nets
dropped with prefabricated instinctual-panic
condensed into unraveling

reveling in the hot climate, sounding off
full-belly snorts in snoring choir
refreshing on lavender pillows of mythos,
laced with mercurial mercy,
pressed on the faceless
as climaxing expressions of taxing charity
fluffing-on from an overhead mirror
binge-replying "will do"
to the greatest story ever retold, reigning
down upon the manger of a glorious preemie
sharing a driptorch ciggie in afterglow finale
as a dropped red ash nestles-in
against the happy animus
shadowbox of drawn-straw figurines
engendered by a spectrum glowing-out
with choiceless ops
awarded for their compromising
core of decency-or-else
with a bouquet of paradise-invasives,
drying in a leased urn,
set up collectively, displayed as unarranged
cuttings from the tangle

3 J Flying Thank Yous

Ending with *J*oshua Bodwell
for sensitivity, time and space,

ongoing with *J*ill Draper
for patience, support and perspective,

and beginning with *J*an Roberts
for teaching with easy-natured acceptance
& encouraging individual discovery
through the freedom of unbridled expression.

PHOTO BY JILL DRAPER

Richard Buckner

b. 1964
N. California
Idaho
Georgia
Washington
Alberta
Texas
New York
d. to some,
(said-mutterer)
crawling along in nonstop flight,
only recently haunching to edit notes
scribbled from subterranean overlooks
in retro-present closing night debut,
circumnavigating theories of trajectory
& other self-assassinating goals
career-graphed in scripted speculation,
rejoiced mounting benign philippics
dodging inkhorned entanglements.

Printed August 2020 in Chelsea, Michigan for the
Black Sparrow Press by Sheridan Books. Set in New
Caledonia by Tammy Ackerman. This first edition
has been bound in paper-over-boards; 100 copies
have been specially bound with cloth spines, and are
numbered and signed by the author.

Black Sparrow Press was founded by John and
Barbara Martin in 1966, and continued by them
until 2002. The iconic sparrow logo was drawn by
Barbara Martin.